Mama Quillo in association with
The Bush Theatre and
Leicester Haymarket Theatre presents

BONES

by Kay Adshead

17 October – 4 November 2006

thebushtheatre

Cast

(in alphabetical order)

Jennifer **Pauline Moran**
Boy / Beauty **Sarah Niles**

With live music by **Joe Legwabe**

Writer and director **Kay Adshead**
Design consultancy **Mike Lees**
Design concept **Mama Quillo**
Lighting design **Lizzie Powell**
Sound design **Sarah Weltman**
Co-sound design **Matt Berry**
Assistant director **Liz Gladwin**
Deputy Stage Manager **Stacey Louise Dixon**
Production / Administration for Mama Quillo **Sue Phelan**
Producer **Angela Sadler**

Press Representation **Alexandra Gammie** 020 7837 8333
Graphic Design **Stem Design** info@stemdesign.co.uk

Mama Quillo is grateful for the support of a project grant from Arts Council, England. Mama Quillo gratefully acknowledges the support of the **bushfutures** Company Mentoring Scheme.

Bones was first workshopped at Leicester Haymarket Theatre in 2005. The play opened in Leicester on 3 October 2006 and received its London première at The Bush Theatre on 17 October 2006.

Pauline Moran *Jennifer*

Theatre includes Mary Tyrone in *Long Day's Journey Into Night*, Vittoria in Country Life, the title role in *No Orchids for Miss Blandish*, Duchess Isabella in *Painter's Palace of Pleasure*, Tanis in *Semi-Monde* (Glasgow Citizen's), Catherine Stockman in *An Enemy of the People* (Bristol Old Vic), Belinda Blair in *Noises Off* (Mobil Touring Theatre), Marlene in *Bitter Tears of Petra von Kant* (Latchmere Theatre), *Little Women, Big Boys* (specially writtten for Pauline by Carol Ann Duffy), *Blood on the Neck of the Cat* (Almeida Theatre), Nicoletta in *Mephisto*, Cassandra in *Troilus and Cressida* (RSC), Miss Wanderley in *Private Dick* (Lyric Hammersmith & Nuffield Southampton), Princess Alais in *The Lion in Winter* (English Theatre Vienna), The Stepdaughter in *Six Characters in Search of an Author* (Greenwich Theatre), Susannah in *Bedroom Farce* (Leeds Playhouse), Beryl in *Sisters* (Royal Exchange Manchester), Vicky & Alice in *Hobson's Choice* (Sheffield Crucible and Colchester Mercury), Shirley in *Sailor Beware*, the title role in *Miss Julie*, Jean in *The Sea Anchor*, Marie in *The Foursome*, Shirley in *The Anniversary*, Jean in *Say Goodnight to Grandma*, Regina in *Ghosts* (Coventry Belgrade), Natasha in *Three Sisters*, Lucy Brown in *The Threepenny Opera* (Watford Palace), Cecily in *The Importance of Being Earnest* (Liverpool Playhouse), Cordelia in *King Lear*, Jenny Beale in *Roots* and Lady Anne in *Richard III* (Liverpool Everyman). **Television** includes Miss Lemon in *Agatha Christie's Poirot* (series 1, 2, 3, 5, 6 and 7), Juliet in *Bugs*, the title role in *The Woman in Black*, Ruby Ray in *Shadow of the Noose*, Empress of Russia in *The Luck Child*, Antoinette de Mauban in *The Prisoner of Zenda*, Cleopatra Berenike in *The Cleopatras*, Helena in *The Trespasser*, Maisie Maidan in *The Good Soldier*, the Teacher in Mike Leigh's *Afternoon*, and many more.

Sarah Niles *Boy / Beauty*

Sarah trained at the Capitol School of Television & Theatre (Manchester Metropolitan University). **Theatre** includes *The Bogus Woman* (Leicester Haymarket, Adelaide Festival, Brits Off Broadway, New York and UK tour; winner of Best Individual Award at the Adelaide Fringe Festival 2006), *The Lion, The Witch and The Wardrobe* and *To Kill A Mockingbird* (Leicester Haymarket), *Legends of the Blues* (Bridewell Theatre), *Entartete Musik* (Denmark tour/London Drill Hall), *Low Down High Notes* (Red Ladder Theatre Company), *Magic Sky, Magic Earth* (Pentabus Theatre Company), *Soho Story* (Young Vic Theatre/UK/Europe), *The Pied Piper* (Kaboodle Theatre Productions), *Black Love* (Black Arts Development Project), *The Caucasian Chalk Circle* (Manchester Library Theatre). **Television** includes *A Touch of Frost*.

Joe Legwabe *Live music*

Joe Legwabe has recorded with many artists including Yusuf Islam (formerly Cat Stevens), Eric Weinrich, The Art Ensemble of Chicago Live with Intombi Zakwazulu (while touring France, Germany, Italy, Monaco and Turkey), The South African Gospel Choir, Yazz, The Art Ensemble of Soweto, Colin James Hay, Paul Young, Manfred Mann, Hugh Masekela, Lena Zavaroni, Ipi Ntombi, Intombi Zesi Manje-Manje, Phuza Ushukela and The Mahlathini Mahotella Queens Makgona Tsohle Band. Movie soundtracks include *The Constant Gardener*, *Sahara*, *Duma*, *The Wild Thorn Berries in Africa* with Peter Gabriel, Sting and the Amabutho and South African Gospel Choirs, and Strander with The Temple of Sound. Joe has toured with many artists, including Ladysmith Black Mambazo, David Murray (UK and European tour, 2001), Ajup Ogada (Mexican tour), Job Seda (Mexican tour), Ayup Uganda (Johannesburg), The Spirit Talk (UK and US tours, plus live recordings), the Moropa Drum Orchestra (UK and European tours) and Shikisha (US Festivals tour). Joe has also performed at *The Brits Music Awards*, on *Tomorrow's World* (BBC), for Hong Kong television with Jackie Chan, at Nelson Mandela concerts (Wembley Stadium and Alexandra Palace), the Montreal Rock Festival in Switzerland, and in Marlon Brando's *A Dry White Season*.

Kay Adshead *Writer and Director*

Kay Adshead's writing work includes *Thatcher's Women* (produced by Paines Plough at the Tricycle Theatre, nominated for the Susan Smith Blackburn Award and published by Methuen), *The Still Born* (Soho Theatre Company), the short play *After The Party* (Altered States at the Liverpool Playhouse and subsequently made into a short Channel 4 film for Club X), *Ravings: Dreamings* (Manchester Library), *Metal and Feathers* (part of *Small Objects of Desire* at the Cockpit Theatre), *Oranges and Lemons* (a short film for BBC City Shorts), *Bacillus* (rehearsed readings at the Cockpit and Hampstead, and performed at the Red Room), *Juicy Bits* (Lyric, Hammersmith), *Lady Chill Lady Wad Lady Love Lady God* (commissioned by the National Theatre as part of BT Connections and performed at the Tricycle and Lyttleton Theatres) and *The Bogus People's Poem* (The Red Room/BAC). Kay has been awarded two Arts Council Theatre Writing Bursaries and in 1995 she received the Calouste Gulbenkian Award Bursary for performance poetry for *The Slug Sabbatical,* performed at the Red Room and published by Faber & Faber. Her play *The Bogus Woman* was produced at the Traverse Theatre, Edinburgh in 2000, where it won a Scotsman Fringe First, and at The Bush Theatre in 2001. It was also broadcast on BBC Radio 3 (produced by Catherine Bailey). The play is published by Oberon Books and was nominated for the 2001 Susan Smith Blackburn

Award. Kay's play for children, *The Snow Egg* (Tiebreak Theatre), toured the UK in 2001 ending at The Lyric Studio, Hammersmith. In Autumn 2002, Kay's latest radio play, *Hanging*, was broadcast on Radio 4 (produced by Catherine Bailey). *Animal* was mounted at the Soho Theatre in September 2003 and then toured the UK. It is published by Oberon Books. *Bites* was performed at The Bush Theatre in 2004–5 and was a finalist for the Susan Smith Blackburn Award. It was developed while Kay was writer in residence at Colchester University. Kay devised and directed with students at East 15 Acting School *A Short (but insightful) Musical History of the British National Party* and for the Guildhall School of Music and Drama *The Jugular Project* (work in progress), an exploration of direct action for 25 actors on a climbing wall. She wrote and acted in *Of The End*, a homage to Samuel Beckett, for Radio 3's *The Verb*. Most recently she has co-devised and written *Others* (work in progress) for London Academy of Music and Dramatic Art, directed by Hannah Eidenow. *Bones* was developed with Lucinda Gane. Kully Thiarai invited Mama Quillo to showcase four performances at the Leicester, Haymarket in October 2005. Kay is about to research a verse play about persistent female offending in HMP Styal and HMP Holloway.

Mike Lees *Design Consultant*

Mike Lees graduated in Theatre Design from the Rose Bruford School of Speech and Drama, having previously worked as an actor, stage-manager, make-up and scenic artist. The range of his work incorporates community theatre, commercial tours, repertory theatre, musicals and operas on varying scales, for London, Europe, America and Russia. Most recently, he has created designs for *What I Heard About Iraq* (Pleasance, Edinburgh), *Gone* (Ambassadors Theatre, London), *Professor Bumm and the Story Machine* (Trafalgar Studios), *Antiphony, All in the Mind, Chinca Chanca Cooroo* (W11 Opera at the Britten Theatre, London), *An Inspector Calls* (for which he won the Mercury Theatre Design Award), *Hayfever, How the Other Half Love* (Little Theatre, Leicester), *Children of Eden, Barnum* (Forum Theatre, New York), *Copacabanna, Chicago, Once Upon A Mattress, Cabaret* (Jack Romano, New York), *Oedipus Tyrannos, Lysistrata* (Bloomsbury Theatre, London), *Whistle Down The Wind* (Churchill Theatre, Bromley & tour), *Sweeney Todd* (Swinburne Hall, Colchester), *Assassins*, the British premiere of Sondheim's *Do I Hear a Waltz?* (Landor, London), *Making History* (Riverside Studios and Irish tour), *The Tempest* (Tudor Barn, Eltham), *Noises Off* (ICA London), *A Doll's House* (Library, Luton) and numerous pantomimes. In the last three years, he has designed and costumed the UK and European tours of several operas, including *Turandot, Madame Butterfly, La Nozze Di Figaro, Don Giozanni, Lulu, La Boheme, Tosca, La Cenrentola, Der Shauspieldirektor, The Fiery Angel* and several Gilbert and Sullivan operettas.

Elizabeth Powell
Lighting Designer

Lighting design work for theatre includes *Drenched* (The Tron, Glasgow / national tour), *The Foolish Man* (Roundhouse Studio), *Vanity Play, The Cudgel and the Rapier, Cowboy Mouth* (BAC), *How to Kill (Your Lover)* (Tron Theatre, Glasgow), *Edinburgh Home Project* (Queen Hall, Edinburgh), *Bones* (Leicester Haymarket Studio), *Making History* (Samuel Beckett Theatre, Dublin), *The Night Shift* (The Esplanade, Singapore and national tour / Traverse, Edinburgh / BAC), *Second City Trilogy* (Cork Opera House), *Romeo & Juliet* (Belvedere College, Dublin / Cork Opera House / The Black Box, Galway), *This Ebony Bird* (Half Moon Theatre, Cork / Irish national tour), *Crave* (national tour), Tricky (Richmond Studio), *A Comedy of Errors* (Globe Theatre, Neuss, Germany), *Patching Havoc* (Latchmere Theatre) and *Howie The Rookie* (Everyman Theatre, Cork). Elizabeth won the NESTA bursary for Lighting Design in 2004, working with Rick Fisher on Britten's opera *A Midsummer Night's Dream* (Venice), *Anna in the Tropics* (Hampstead Theatre) and *Billy Elliot* (West End). Other theatre work includes *The Evocation of Papa Maas* (Assistant Lighting Designer, national tour), *Billy Elliot* (Assistant to Lighting Designer, West End), *Paliagio* (Re-lights and Technical Manager, national tour), *Animal* (Re-lights and Technical Manager, national tour), *Mnemonic* (Production Assistant, international tour), *Carmen* (Re-lights and Technical Manager, national tour) and *The Noise of Time* (Student Production Assistant, international tour). Elizabeth is Artistic Director of Blood In The Alley Theatre Company, Ireland.

Sarah Weltman *Sound Designer*

As well as working for Mama Quillo on the first production of *Bones* last year at Leicester Haymarket and previously on *Bites* at The Bush Theatre, Sarah's sound designs include *The Time Of The Tortoise* (Theatre 503), *Summer Begins* (Southwark Playhouse), *The Mouse Queen* (New Victory Theatre, New York), *Over Gardens Out* (Southwark Playhouse) and *Bread and Butter* (Tricycle Theatre); also Assistant Sound Designer on the recent West End revival of *One Flew Over The Cuckoo's Nest* at The Garrick. For the Young Vic Theatre where Sarah is currently Sound Manager – *Six Characters Looking For An Author, A Night At The Circus* (PUSH), *Red Demon*, and as part of Direct Action Season *Winners, Interior, The Exception And The Rule* and *The New Tenant*. For Y Touring Theatre Company – *Every Breath* (National Tour and Edinburgh Fringe), *Headstone* (Arcola Theatre), *Mind The Gap, The Gift, Wasted* and *Pig In The Middle, Mr Elliot* (Chelsea Theatre). For Dukes Playhouse, Lancaster – *The BFG, How The Other Half Loves, The Ugly Duckling, Driving Miss Daisy* and *American Buffalo*.

Liz Gladwin *Assistant Director*

Liz Gladwin trained as an actor at the Centre For Performing Arts. She has since worked with Annon Productions, Zip Antics and The Rude Mechanicals as an actor, and Scylla Productions and Vitalstatistix: National Women's Theatre as a Director and Director's Assistant. Next year she will be Urban Myth: Theatre of Youth's featured emerging director.

Mama Quillo

(Co-Producer)

Mama Quillo is a women-led theatre company. Kay Adshead and Lucinda Gane created the company to offer a uniquely female perspective on the really big issues of the day. Angela Sadler, a lawyer with experience in the voluntary sector on human rights issues, became company director shortly after.

Their first co-production *The Bogus Woman* looked at what it is really like to seek asylum in this country. It won a Fringe First, was nominated for an E.M.M.A. and The Susan Smith Blackburn Award. The actress Noma Dumezweni won the Manchester Evening News for Best Fringe Performance. It has twice toured the U.K. and was broadcast on BBC Radio 3. In translation it has had acclaimed productions in France, Spain, Belgium and Equatorial Guinea. Most recently in a Leicester Haymarket production, playing New York and Adelaide Fringe Festival, Sarah Niles won Best Performance out of 4,000 performers and the play won The Sunsation Award.

Mama Quillo's second production *Bites*, about Texas and Afghanistan and researched with help from RAWA (Revolutionary Association of the Women of Afghanistan), played The Bush Theatre and was a finalist in The Susan Smith Blackburn Award. *Bites*, in translation, is currently being produced in Portugal.

Bones is about South Africa in 2006. It was developed with Lucinda Gane and Sarah Niles and showcased at the Leicester Haymarket in 2005. The parts of Jennifer and Beauty were written for them. Tragically, Lucinda died before playing the part, but *Bones* is a testament to her extraordinary spirit.

Angela Sadler is now Executive Producer and Kay Adshead Artistic Director. Our outreach work includes workshops for The Crossroads Women's Centre in Kentish Town with asylum seekers and voluntary workers, with whom we have created short street theatre performance pieces. Most recently we hosted, with the Women's Action Network, a benefit performance at the Human Rights Action Centre to raise money for legal advice sessions for asylum seekers.

We contributed a workshop performance of 'Ice Cream' from *Bites* at the 'Stop Violence Against Women' forum for the Women's Action Network and Amnesty, and have contributed to the Women in Exile Conference in Oxford and London. We are currently organizing 'Buried Pasts' workshops, exploring personal and social histories.

Mama Quillo is a South American lunar goddess, a harbinger of change, and our slogan is 'Theatre For Change'. Our future plans include a verse play, researched inside HMP Styal and HMP Holloway, about persistent female offenders.

The Bush Theatre

(Co-Producer)

'One of the most experienced prospectors of raw talent in Europe' *The Independent*

The Bush Theatre is one of the most celebrated new writing theatres in the world. We have an international reputation for discovering, nurturing and producing the best new theatre writers from the widest range of backgrounds, and for presenting their work to the highest possible standards. We look for exciting new voices that tell contemporary stories with wit, style and passion and we champion work that is both provocative and entertaining.

With around 40,000 people enjoying our productions each year, The Bush has produced hundreds of ground-breaking premieres since its inception 34 years ago. The theatre produces up to eight productions of new plays a year, many of them Bush commissions, and hosts guest productions by leading companies and artists from all over the world.

The Bush is widely acclaimed as the seedbed for the best new playwrights, many of whom have gone on to become established names in the entertainment industry, including Steve Thompson, Jack Thorne, Amelia Bullmore, Dennis Kelly, Chloë Moss, David Eldridge, Stephen Poliakoff, Snoo Wilson, Terry Johnson, Kevin Elyot, Doug Lucie, Dusty Hughes, Sharman Macdonald, Billy Roche, Catherine Johnson, Philip Ridley, Richard Cameron, Jonathan Harvey, Conor McPherson, Joe Penhall, Helen Blakeman, Mark O'Rowe and Charlotte Jones. We also champion the introduction of new talent to the industry, whilst continuing to attract major acting and directing talents, including Richard Wilson, Nadim Sawalha, Bob Hoskins, Alan Rickman, Antony Sher, Stephen Rea, Frances Barber, Lindsay Duncan, Brian Cox, Kate Beckinsale, Patricia Hodge, Simon Callow, Alison Steadman, Jim Broadbent, Tim Roth, Jane Horrocks, Mike Leigh, Mike Figgis, Mike Newell, Victoria Wood and Julie Walters.

The Bush has won over one hundred awards, and developed an enviable reputation for touring its acclaimed productions nationally and internationally. Recent tours and transfers include a national number one tour of *Mammals* (2006), an international tour of *After The End* (2005–6), *adrenalin...heart* representing the UK in the Tokyo International Arts Festival (2004), the West End transfer (2002) and national tour of *The Glee Club* (2004), a European tour of *Stitching* (2003) and Off-Broadway transfers of *Howie the Rookie* and *Resident Alien*. Film adaptations include *Beautiful Thing* and *Disco Pigs*.

The Bush Theatre provides a free script reading service, receiving over 1500 scripts through the post every year, and reading them all. This is one small part of a comprehensive **Writers' Development Programme**, which includes workshops, one-to-one dramaturgy, rehearsed readings, research bursaries, masterclasses, residencies and commissions. We have also launched a pilot scheme for an ambitious new education, training and professional development programme, **bushfutures**, providing opportunities for different sectors of the community and professionals to access the expertise of Bush writers, directors, designers, technicians and actors, and to play an active role in influencing the future development of the theatre and its programme.

The Bush Theatre is extremely proud of its reputation for artistic excellence, its friendly atmosphere, and its undisputed role as a major force in shaping the future of British theatre.

Mike Bradwell Artistic Director • **Fiona Clark** Executive Producer

At The Bush Theatre

Artistic Director	**Mike Bradwell**
Executive Producer	**Fiona Clark**
Finance Manager	**Dave Smith**
Literary Manager	**Abigail Gonda**
Marketing Manager	**Nicki Marsh**
Production Manager	**Robert Holmes**
Theatre Administrator	**Nic Wass**
Resident Stage Manager	**Ros Terry**
Acting Literary Assistant	**Raphael Martin**
Administrative Assistant	**Lydia Fraser-Ward**
Box Office Supervisor	**Darren Elliott**
Box Office Assistants	**Gail MacLeod, Margaret-Ann Bain**
Front of House Duty Managers	**Kellie Batchelor, Adrian Christopher, Siobhan King-Spooner, Glenn Mortimer, Catherine Nix-Collins, Lois Tucker**
Duty Technicians	**Jonathan Goldstone, Tom White, Sean Wilkinson**
Associate Artists	**Tanya Burns, Es Devlin, Richard Jordan, Paul Miller**
Pearson Playwright in Residence	**Jack Thorne**
Press Representative	**Alexandra Gammie** 020 7837 8333

The Bush Theatre
Shepherds Bush Green
London W12 8QD
Box Office: 020 7610 4224
www.bushtheatre.co.uk

The Alternative Theatre Company Ltd. (The Bush Theatre)
is a Registered Charity number: 270080
Co. registration number 1221968
VAT no. 228 3168 73

Be there at the beginning

The Bush Theatre is a writer's theatre – exclusively dedicated to commissioning, developing and producing new plays. Up to seven writers each year are commissioned and we offer a bespoke programme of workshops and one-to-one dramaturgy to develop their plays. Our international reputation of over thirty years is built on consistently producing the very best work to the very highest standard.

With your help this work can continue to flourish.

The Bush Theatre's Patron Scheme delivers an exciting range of opportunities for individual and corporate giving, offering a closer relationship with the theatre and a wide range of benefits from ticket offers to special events. Above all, it is an ideal way to acknowledge your support for one of the world's greatest new writing theatres.

To join, please pick up an information pack from the foyer, call 020 7602 3703 or email info@bushtheatre.co.uk

We would like to thank our current members and invite you to join them!

Lone Star
Princess of Darkness

Handful of Stars
Gianni Alen-Buckley

Glee Club
Anonymous
Jim Broadbent
Adam Kenwright
Curtis Brown Group Ltd
Richard & Elizabeth Philipps
Alan Rickman

Beautiful Thing
Anonymous
Alan Brodie
Kate Brooke
David Brooks
Clive Butler
Matthew Byam Shaw
Jeremy Conway
Clyde Cooper
Anna Donald
Mike Figgis
Vivien Goodwin
Sheila Hancock
David Hare
Bill Keeling
Laurie Marsh
Michael McCoy
John & Jacqui Pearson

Mr & Mrs A Radcliffe
Wendy Rawson
John Reynolds
David Pugh & Dafydd Rogers
Barry Serjent
John & Tita Shakeshaft
Brian D Smith
Barrie & Roxanne Wilson

Rookies
Anonymous
Ross Anderson
Pauline Asper
Lady Constance Byam Shaw
Geraldine Caufield
Nigel Clark
Nina Drucker
Ms Sian Hansen
Lucy Heller
Mr G Hopkinson
Joyce Hytner, ACT IV
Robert Israel for Gordon & Co.
Hardeep Kalsi
Casarotto Ramsay &
Associates Ltd
Robin Kermode
Ray Miles
Mr & Mrs Malcolm Ogden
Radfin
Clare Rich
Mark Roberts

David Robinson
Tracey Scoffield
Councillor Minnie Scott Russell
Martin Shenfield
Loveday Waymouth
Alison Winter

**Platinum Corporate
Membership**
Anonymous

**Silver Corporate
Membership**
The Agency (London) Ltd

**Bronze Corporate
Membership**
Anonymous
The Peters, Fraser & Dunlop
Group Ltd
Act Productions Ltd

BONES

was developed with,
written for,
and is dedicated to
Lucinda Gane.
It celebrates her indomitable heart.

First published in 2006 by Oberon Books Ltd.
521 Caledonian Road, London N7 9RH
Tel: 020 7607 3637 / Fax: 020 7607 3629
e-mail: info@oberonbooks.com
www.oberonbooks.com

A catalogue record for this book is available from the British Library.

ISBN: 1 84002 689 8 / 978-1-84002-689-4

Cover image: Stem Design

Printed in Great Britain by Antony Rowe Ltd, Chippenham.

Production Notes

The circumstances surrounding the writing and producing of *Bones* have been unusual and dramatic.

I founded Mama Quillo with Lucinda Gane, who was my close friend for 20 years. We met as actresses in rep, I had always loved her work, and I looked forward, at some point, to writing for her. In *Bites*, our second production, I created a line of challenging parts around her, notably L in 'Ice Cream', the fifth of seven short plays.

But in July 2004 Lucinda was diagnosed with terminal cancer and given 18 months to live. It is an understatement to say this came as a shock. Lucinda's course of chemotherapy meant she would miss the first week of rehearsal for *Bites*, so, typically, she decided that the best thing was to drop out of the acting, but continue producing, with myself. Which she did, doing more than her fair share of the donkey work.

After the chemotherapy, and with *Bites* now finished at The Bush, Lucinda rallied.

I wondered if she had one more performance in her.

I had wanted to write a play about South Africa, after The Truth and Reconciliation Commission had long gone, for years. Lucinda had left South Africa to train at RADA, and her sister, Gill Gane, had been part of the struggle against apartheid, resulting in her deportation.

Using them both as primary sources (as well as others more bang up to date) I decided to write my play.

I wanted it to be hopeful, not another play about race hatred violence. I wanted it to be about the black South African population's astonishing willingness to reinvent their society, after the holocaust of apartheid. I felt, in this age of threats, retribution and revenge, they were an example to the so-called first world.

I decided to write a two-hander for Lucinda and Sarah Niles – a shining young black actress who had played the Bogus Woman in my play of that name at The Haymarket, Leicester.

Kully Thiarai had directed that production (with great integrity) and she invited me to take a first draft of the new play *Bones* to Leicester for four performances in October 2005.

I wrote three or four scenes at a time. We would convene around Lucinda's kitchen table, read and then discuss.

Lucinda and Sarah had the kind of rapport that exists between two really good actors working together, who respect and really like each other, and are interested in looking out for each other. For me, it was bliss.

Lucinda's beautiful bald head was replaced by surprising Harpo Marx curls – and we proceeded with hope.

I finished the play in late July 2005, not too far from our mooted September rehearsal.

Lucinda, looking a little frail, organised a reading of the final draft around the kitchen table, with Christopher, her husband as audience. She was, as always, the perfect hostess, albeit with one arm out of commission because of the cancer!

But more to the point she was utterly astonishing that afternoon as Jennifer. I wish we had taped it. Very sadly, and like something out of the play itself, it was her last acting performance.

Lucinda's sudden, and dramatic, decline took her first to the Middlesex Hospital and then to the Marie Curie Hospice.

Her life in those end weeks was simply extraordinary.

We, all her friends, would set out (me from rehearsing *Bones*) full of fear, only to find Lucinda, unexpectedly, radiant. We enjoyed all the usual titbits – baby bottles of champagne, perfect, black shiny cherries, best Russian vodka, blinis and caviar – around her bed, and we would all leave more cheerful than we arrived.

She was bald again and, cheerfully, all-knowing. It was like visiting the Dalai Lama.

The production opened in Leicester. Lucinda held on, suddenly battling and ferocious, in the hospice until the first night, and with her actress's perfect timing passed away the next morning.

In this production in October/November 2006, Pauline Moran, Lucinda's friend of 35 years, and a member of our Advisory Board, plays Jennifer. We had discussed this possibility and it become important to us in Lucinda's last weeks. Pauline has made Jennifer utterly her own.

Lucinda also bequeathed me Angie Sadler to take the post of Executive Producer in Mama Quillo, knowing that I like women with very loud laughs.

As well as being a wonderful actress, Lucinda was the most decent human being I have ever known. I hope this play and all future Mama Quillo plays honour her.

K A

Cast

BOY / BEAUTY
Young Black Woman

JENNIFER
White Woman, late 50s

SINGER / DRUMMER / PERCUSSIONIST
The voice of the Isinyanya

The play is performed from the beginning in the pit. The bed is suggested by four bagged up rose bushes. All around are other rose bushes in bags, some are as high as 25 foot, supported by canes. The bags are suggestive of bags of bones – or body bags. Others, the tall ones, cast shadows that suggest the Isinyanya.

Boy and Beauty must be played by the same female performer. The boy does not leave the performing space until the end of Scene 6. Jennifer remains on stage during all the Boy's scenes.

All characters are South African.

The play is set in present day Johannesburg, apart from the Boy's scenes with the Interrogator which are set in 1969.

As audience enter, on tape, a little girl, perhaps a 10-year-old Beauty is singing and dissolving into laughter; interspersed is the live drumming, urgent and disconcerting.

In the Boy's scenes, the symbol ❖ is used to indicate points at which his interrogator speaks, unheard by the audience.

Scene 1

Breath.

Singing – terrible, beautiful. The Isinyanya call to the bones.

A young black BOY (aged 17) – his hands are tied behind his back, his legs are bound at the ankle.

He is lit as by a torch from the front. He is being interrogated.

BOY

I don't know
twenty maybe
twenty at first

❖

Yes
didn't I just
tell you
Baas?

❖

Water,
about the water
mainly,
other things of course,
but a child
had died
drinking
from the tap
they thought,

so

they called
a meeting.

❖

The leaders

❖

The leaders
of the Residents Association

❖

More agitated.

You know

who they are,
everyone knows.

It's no secret
who they are

❖

Of course I know her,
I am
her son.

I am
her son

❖

No!
I don't know
that person

❖

No
I don't know
his name

❖

I…

❖

I have
never
met him!

❖

All the people

❖

Yes
the residents
they…

❖

Spilled

❖

Yes, they spilled out,
onto the football pitch

❖

Twenty at the meeting
but outside

there were…

others.

❖

Just others
other people

❖

At first,
they were all
young men

❖

I don't know,
maybe
a hundred

❖

Of course
I remember exactly
what they were doing

They were singing
and dancing
that's all

small boys
climbed
onto their brother's backs

bouncing
up and down
in fun

And one
old man,
thin as sticks,
rode his grandson
like a mule,
banging tins
like drums,
baring his gums
and laughing –
And so
they clapped
all of them
and danced

And some of them
they sang
Baas

Terrified.

Why am I here?
Why
have you brought me
here?

to this

terrible

terrible

place?

For the first time his eyes acknowledge two other men present.

I told you
everything, mybasé
at the police station

He looks up.

What
are you doing?

Truly,
I have nothing
to tell you

Truly.

Scene 2

Lights change to soft lamplight.
An elegant slim blonde woman in her 50s wearing a cream silk yele enters.
She addresses exactly the same spot as the BOY.

JENNIFER

Brightly.

Pieter?

A rattle from the drums.

I thought
I thought
I heard you call
darling

I fell asleep
on the couch.
Disastrous!
Means
I won't sleep
tonight.

Not a wink.

She moves over to her husband's bedside and looks down at him.

Softer still.

Can you
hear me?

I think
you can

Suddenly animated.

Did I tell you?

Softer.

Did I?

Four aces
and still I lost!

I partnered Dot
who was wearing
a dress
a size too small
and who
managed to fidget all
the way through
the first four hands

Myra wouldn't stop
yakking
I don't mean to be…cruel…
on and on
about
that foolish son
of hers

Ed's graduated
from Joburg Gen

But instead
of practising oncology
and then
quite possibly
saving lives

he's decided
to make novelty lamps
out of rock salt
and sell them
over the internet

Rubbing her shoulders.

Why is it
so cold
in here?

Oh, and I
didn't tell you
about
Steve and Dottie's
pool –

mosaics of Neptune
I ask you
fish tail
and a trident.
They'll be the laughing stock.

Pause.

Everyone
asked after you
darling

I said
no visitors
not now
I told them
we'd discussed it
with the doctors
we'd agreed

Pause.

Rubbing her shoulders.

the nurse
knows
you hate
the cold.

End of July
he'd always
light a fire
I said
always

Pause.

Very, very soft.

I had a dream
dozing
on the couch.

A curious dream.

*At intervals – and very, very softly – drums
underscore.*

I'm five
four or five.

It's noon
and the
sun
is
high
and hot

I'm in
the shade
of
a tree,

digging
in the
red
earth

with a

stolen
kitchen knife.

Mummy's
inside,
baking

a
sponge cake
for tea

If
she saw
the knife
she'd be cross

I've made
a hole,

and

I'm
pouring water
from a
plastic
tea pot
to make
mud pies.

Suddenly

in my
murky
little well

something...

flutters...
and
splashes...

It is
a
butterfly

drowning!

I wonder
how it
got inside
my
mud
hole.

I

kneel
and lift
the beautiful
butterfly

onto the
sharp
blade,

hold it

up

to let

it dry,

hoping it

will fly

away –

And
as I
do so,
I see
in the
far
distance

against
the sky

on the
rusty
hillside

two figures

watching me;

warriors –

The drums signify their appearance.

a man
and a
fierce
robed woman
with a spear

Two figures
so tiny
they can
stand
on the blade
of the
muddy kitchen
knife

with the
giant butterfly

bronzy-blue
again
and brilliant

and
just about
ready
to flutter off,

when –

something else

bubbles

in

the

brown

mud,

bubbles
and
foams
and froths,

something…

bigger.

I hear
Mummy
behind me
running
over
the hot
dry grass

and I

feel a

scream
like a
shard
of glass

in my
throat

and

the warriors
stand
suddenly
over me

and

and

then...

Drumming stops.

Scene 3

*The BOY is kneeling sideways, his head is at a strange
angle, his hands still tied behind his back, his feet
still tied. The BOY's eyes are glazed, his mouth froths
blood. He breathes shallowly.*

BOY
They started
To shoot

❖

He laughs.

Who
do you think?

❖

The police
Started to shoot
The BOY breathes.

❖

He mumbles.
Into the air

❖

Into the air!
Into the air!
The BOY starts to tremble, to whimper.

❖

Yes...
many people
many people
gathering

❖

Children,
women with babies
tied to their backs,
old sick men
with sticks.

❖

Why?

❖

I don't know why.
They heard
the singing
and dancing
I suppose.

❖

No.
No one told
them to go
there

❖

I hid
in the backroom
of a shop

❖

Yes
behind a sack
of mealie meal

He laughs.

by a tower of
Illovo golden syrup tins,
two fell on my toes –
heavy, those tins.

❖

I didn't
have to hide

I...

I...

❖

I was scared
of the shooting
and shouting

I thought
it would
only last
a few hours
perhaps

Then
I could go home

But
It went
on and on

I heard
feet running
screams
then groans

at last
it was
very quiet
and
I stepped out

❖

Yes
from behind
the mealie
meal

I pushed
open
the door

It creaked.

I saw
a small group
looking down
at something
on the ground

I knew
one of them
as my friend.

❖

Distressed.

I…

❖

I…

Almost shouting.

Xolite!
he is called
Xolite!

When I approached
they moved apart

❖

I
saw
lying on the ground

smashed
and bloody

the old man
the oupa
with the grinning gums
banging his tin can drums

And I knew
this
was a very bad thing

because
all the people
the many people

would
be angry

when they saw
the broken body
of this poor
old man.

❖

Panting, very distressed.
Am I, Baas?
Am I doing well?

❖

Yes..
A very
big crowd
now

❖

Yes
Silent yes

❖

No singing
and
no dancing
baas

❖

No, I
knew
no one

❖

Yes
but not by me
I never
threw
a stone

❖

No!
I didn't
organise baas
No.
I couldn't
I wouldn't
Please baas.

My head
is hurting

Please baas
My eyes
Please…

He starts to cry.

Mama

I want my mother
Can I go home now?

She makes me
hot bean pot
on Mondays.

My baby sister
worries
if I'm late

Please…
I have
to go
to be
with my
sisi

Please
Have you
No one
you love
Baas?

Scene 4

*JENNIFER is seated at Pieter's bedside. She is stirring
a crystal tumbler of warm milk and whisky. She has
one of Pieter's large cashmere jumpers draped around
her shoulders, and sometimes she strokes this.*

JENNIFER
Very soft.
I saw you
standing
in the frame
of the door

a shadow

I shivered

*Drums. The BOY is being kicked, he gasps, flinches
and rolls.*

It's very strange,

and it can't
be true,

but apart
from Dad
and Johnson

you're the only man
I remember
as a child

standing

on the patio
at sunset.

Janey came
racing down
to meet me

yelling
that we'd been burgled –

again,

'cept this time
they'd taken
our christening mugs
and our
silver frame
baby pictures,

and Mother
was crying.

And
you stood there
drying

your hands
on the
dishcloth

The one
with the words
and the picture of daffodils

'I wandered, lonely as a cloud
That floats on high…'

looking so handsome
in your uniform
strong
but shy,
I remember.

Anyway,

looking
like a man should
Mother said
grudgingly
long after

A real man.

Janey said
your eyebrows
were too bushy

and you smelled funny

Cigar smoke
I suppose

And she didn't
like policemen.

Anyway
I knew
when you smiled

that you were mine
and mine only.

And it didn't matter to me
that I was thirteen
and you were an old man
of twenty-three.

Drum rattle.

Looking at him.

She stands.

Are you trying
to wake
Pieter?

Drum rattle.

Are you trying
to speak?

Shall I get
the nurse
darling?

Pause.

No?
Just a bad dream.

Pause.

She paces.

You wouldn't
kiss me
till I was sixteen
remember?

On my sixteenth
birthday

we drove
down to Linksfield Ridge.

It was coming to dusk
and hot
we got out of the car

You held my hand
I was embarrassed
because I thought
It was...well...
damp
probably,
sweaty.

You sat me down
on a stump

of an

old fig tree

You knelt
and I could feel
my heart
pump and swell

and

from your back
trouser pocket
you took out
a dainty
heart-shaped box

opened it

and there
was a
gold ring

with the
tiniest diamond,

a fairy tear
you said,
a happy tear.

You put

it on
my finger

and asked
me to be
your fairy wife.

You kissed me
very gently
on the lips

And I said
'Yes, Pieter'

and you put
your head
in my lap

you wept, darling

and I stroked
your brown bear
hair

And I lifted
your great head
like a stone
in my hands

And you kissed
me again,

but this time

you kissed
me
very hard.

You said
we'd have
to wait
of course

that the
whole world
would be
angry
with us

but that…

resistance…

would make
it all the better
in the end

Drums.

Pause.

all the better

Three slow drum beats, a drip, drip, drip

Scene 5

Darkness. A single spot of light. The BOY is hanging.
He can hardly be seen. He can hardly speak. He is
alone. Slow drumbeats throughout are a slow drip,
drip.

BOY

His voice is husky, his words slurred.

Gone?

Have they

gone?

No…

I hear them

out there

finding wood

for a fire

are they?

Someone digging?

The earth

will be

hard

and red.

I once

planted

a

Dombeya Tree

helping my

uncle

In a fine

white woman's

garden

I liked

the

forest lilies

with petals

like

dog's ears

or
tears

the
aloes
which
bleed
white ooze
when you
squeeze

I liked
the creepers
with their
million
tiny blue
stars

One day
I would
like
to be
a gardener

like

my uncle

one day

Pause.

Someone has entered. He looks about.

Who's there?

A girl

Is it?

A young
woman
anyway?

Help me
please

Help me?

Scene 6

JENNIFER is standing holding her empty cup, still addressing the bed. In the background, the growl of mechanical diggers. Still the slow soft intermittent drip…drip drumbeat.

JENNIFER

No
No
that's unacceptable

BOY

Help me

JENNIFER

I told them

After 7 a m
I'd tolerate
but
not before

BOY

Cut me
down

JENNIFER

not a second
not a millisecond

'My husband's
sick'
I said
'very sick

he mustn't
be disturbed'

BOY

Help me

JENNIFER

'by diggers
and workmen'

and you know
these people
a motley gang
will congregate
no doubt

on the other side
of the fence

or, worse still
outside the gate.

To stare
and...

sing perhaps
and…and…

BOY
Untie
my hands

JENNIFER
It's awful
just too
…

BOY
My feet

She pulls herself together.

She goes over to the bed, speaking softly.

JENNIFER
Darling,

they're digging
up the
rose garden

today.

You mustn't
fret

Tsogo funerals
have been
given a
permit
apparently

to dig
for their

ancestors' graves

Under breath.

Why they have
to be
under our rose garden
I don't know.

Pause.

Why couldn't
they be
under
Steve and Dottie's
pool?

Anyway
it won't take long.

a couple of days
no more.

All the roses
have been
dug up
already

tagged
labelled
fed and watered

They said
they'd put
them back

exactly as before.

You know
how strict
I am
with planting

the border
of polyanthas
scrolled and frilled
pink as flesh

Charles de Mills
in the middle
blood-red and bursting

BOY

Help me

JENNIFER

The bower of
Félicité and Perpetué
takes the eye
with their double pompoms
flushed and dewy

down to the
stone folly
the lemon grove

the walled white garden,
and the
tennis courts.

Only a couple
of days

darling

that's all

a couple
of days
digging.

*The dripping finally stops. Drumming and singing,
the Isinyanya welcome the bones.*

Scene 7

*Early morning. JENNIFER sits, as before, on the
small seat at Pieter's bedside, sideways on now, no
longer looking at him. She is singing an old Scottish
lament, rather soft, sweet and girlish. She seems far
away.*

In the near distance, the sound of mechanical diggers.

BEAUTY enters, dressed in a maid's uniform.

BEAUTY
Good morning, Mrs Joubert

JENNIFER jumps.

JENNIFER
Miriam
I…
I didn't
hear you
dear.

BEAUTY
I'm not
Miriam
Mrs Joubert

JENNIFER
Not Miriam?

BEAUTY
No
I'm Beauty.

JENNIFER
Really?

BEAUTY
Yes

JENNIFER
And
have we
met?

BEAUTY
Laughs.
Many times
Mrs Joubert
I've worked
here
seven and a half months

JENNIFER
Seven months

BEAUTY
Yes
just before
the baas
got ill

JENNIFER
I see

BEAUTY
My first day
was
Mr Joubert's
70th birthday
'brunchtime bash'

JENNIFER
Was it?
I…

BEAUTY
I served boerewors
and
herby mash

JENNIFER
I'm afraid
I can't remember

BEAUTY
My friend
Honor
Was on
Buck's fizz

she can smile
but without teeth

so

Jeffrey switched us
'cos I smile good
with plenty teeth

She smiles.

JENNIFER
The pretty
chatty
little girl…

BEAUTY
With the big smile…

JENNIFER
Yes
I remember now

BEAUTY
You gave me
a blanket
Mrs Joubert,
very kindly,
months ago,
pink and woolly
for my sister's
baby
who
by the way
says thank you

JENNIFER
But where's
Miriam?

BEAUTY
Miriam
has left
to go
to college

She wants
to be
a vet.

JENNIFER
Really?
Extraordinary
Miriam –
a vet!

BEAUTY
Anyway
an
animal
nurse.

A strange
vocation
I know
for a girl
who can't
abide
a
spider

or a
cockroach
or a songalolo

but then
spiders
never get
sick.

JENNIFER
Smiling.
Don't they?

BEAUTY
No
they get
trod on
very often,

but never
sick.

A spider
is either

alive
or
dead.

And
they never

need
a vet.

Pause.

JENNIFER
Why
are you
here?

BEAUTY
Why?

JENNIFER
Yes now,
here now.

BEAUTY
To change
Mr Joubert's
bed linen

JENNIFER
On your own.
You come
into
my husband's
room
every day
alone?

BEAUTY
I don't
come
in alone,

No

I'm waiting
for
Nurse Helen.

We have
to change
the bed sheets
before
the doctors
come
at eight.

JENNIFER
I see,
of course.

Pause.

BEAUTY
When they
didn't
find you
in your
room,

everyone
went
hunting.

I knew
You'd be
in here
with Baas.

JENNIFER
How?

BEAUTY
I knew

BEAUTY looks around.

Are all
these photos
you and Baas?

JENNIFER
Yes
we're very young.

BEAUTY
Referring to one.
You look
happy

JENNIFER
That was taken
on our honeymoon
in France.

BEAUTY
Referring to another.
That's funny.

JENNIFER
My
naughty nephews
buried him
in sand.

BEAUTY
And all
your pretty things?

Carvings
and
paintings

JENNIFER
I collect,

Pause.

Do
you like
the house?

BEAUTY
I like
it
very much

JENNIFER
I designed
the interior
myself

with help
of course

to set off
our many
treasures

The style
is
African Zen

That's
what it's
called

BEAUTY
I like
this style

when I have
my own home

I too
will fill it
with pretty things
like you.

JENNIFER

Will you?

A pause.

BEAUTY

With
African Zen

Pause.

Millie May
sent me
to say

she'd put
your tray on
the
first floor
balcony,

that way
you don't
see
the diggers
Mrs Joubert.

JENNIFER

That's very
thoughtful
of Millie
thank her

BEAUTY turns to go.

Ask Millie
to tell me
when
they plan
to leave
will you?

BEAUTY

Leave?

JENNIFER

The workmen
and
the diggers.

I want
to know
the minute

they plan
to go.

BEAUTY
I know that
Mrs Joubert.

They will
stop digging
when
they find

the
Isinyanya

The drum roll repeats Isinyanya.

Pause.

JENNIFER
I'm sorry?

BEAUTY
Our old people
who lie
beneath
the soil.

Pause.

JENNIFER
Agitated.
Really
this is…
this is…
unbearable.

Don't they know
how ill
my husband is?

Couldn't they
have waited
out of common
decency.
a day or two –
couldn't they –
a week.

BEAUTY
They have waited
a long time

Mrs Joubert
the Isinyanya,

The drum repeats Isinyanya.

a very very
long time.

Pause.

JENNIFER
Calmer.
Are there
people gathered
there?

BEAUTY
Yes

JENNIFER
And watching?

BEAUTY
Yes

My mother,
sister
and brother

all are watching
happily
outside the fence.

Also cousins
uncles and aunts
who have
travelled far
from Soweto

They are in
their best frocks
and hats,
the men in suits

I made them
sandwiches

And they
have brought
reed mats
to sit on

cold drinks

and a pack
of ginger nuts.

JENNIFER looks at her, incredulous, for a long time.

She laughs.

BEAUTY
Alarmed.
Do you need
a
Doctor
Mrs Joubert?

JENNIFER
Don't tell me,
Dr Haines
is sitting
downstairs in
Millie's kitchen
tucking into
one of her
famous
English
fry-ups.

BEAUTY
He had
eggs
this morning

I believe

and smoked haddock
on buttery brown toast

a pot of coffee
and three
Marie biscuits.
Oh, and one naartjie,
He spits the pips
into
his empty coffee cup.

JENNIFER
Smiling.
You are
a funny little girl.

BEAUTY
Thank you.

JENNIFER
Tell Millie,

everyone

I'll be

a few minutes

will you?

BEAUTY

Yes, Mrs Joubert.

BEAUTY makes to go then stops, turns back.

They also
have bibles
as well
as the ginger nuts
and cold drinks.

JENNIFER looks puzzled.

My family –
and precious
family things

photos

like yours

Mrs Joubert

and certificates
and songs.

JENNIFER

I…
I didn't
mean
to be
disrespectful
of course.

BEAUTY

They'll sing,
to welcome
the
Isinyanya –

Drum repeats Isinyanya.

who may
scream,
when torn
from the
dark red soil
and flung
into the sunlight.

They'll sing
and dance
to soothe
the spirits.

The bones
of the
Isinyanya

Drum repeats Isinyanya.

will be lifted
put in bags
and carried
careful
to the trucks

And

in these
troubled hours
back
in the air

with their
spirits
free to roam

they will visit
their
children's, children's
children

and they
in turn
will bring
their babes,
the young
and fat,
and the
old men
with sticks
too
will tell
their tales.

And so
the spirits
of the

Isinyanya

Drum repeats Isinyanya.

Will be

amongst
us.

All of us.

It is
a
dangerous
time.

JENNIFER
Dangerous?

BEAUTY
Yes
you see
they may be
angry.

JENNIFER
That's…
preposterous.

BEAUTY
Perhaps.

Angry
to be
disturbed

from their
sleep
beneath the soil.

JENNIFER
Who told you
all this…?

BEAUTY
Nobody
told me

It is
the way
it is,
you see
I have the caul
I was born
at the very hour
my grandfather
died.

My Xhosa name

means
'forefathers' voice'

I speak
to the spirits,
and sometimes
in dreams,
or in strange
waking moments
when the world
stops and spins,
they kindly
speak to me.

Pause.

JENNIFER

Agitated.

You shouldn't
say those things
not in here
not now
it's…

BEAUTY

I spoke to
Zandile's grandma
the other day
Zandile was grateful
for she
loved her gran
who died
and never said
goodbye.

She baked me
a pumpkin pie
and gave me a big comb
on a string
made of plastic sparkly stuff
to wear
around my neck.

She smiles.

Zandile
that is
not
her gran
Nomse's babe

came through
to me,

her stillborn
babe

who told me
to tell her mama
to plant white daisies
on her little grave

which she did.

You see
I made
her happy.

She stopped
taking pills
from the Doctor
and paid me
fifty rand
in three clean
and crispy bills.

Pause.

JENNIFER
Do you always
receive payment?

Pause.

BEAUTY
Always

JENNIFER
I see.

BEAUTY
It honours
the spirits.

Also
Mrs Joubert
I have
the power
to heal.

JENNIFER
Yes

BEAUTY
White people
in their big

shiny cars
drive
many kilometres
with their sickness
which I heal.

Pause.

JENNIFER
What…
sickness?

BEAUTY
Sickness of the mind,
of the body,
especially –
limbs, lungs
and liver

and
of the soul

I charge
a bit more
for the soul.

JENNIFER
Listen

There is silence.

The diggers
have stopped.

Drum. BEAUTY takes out an apple, which she eats.

Scene 8

BEAUTY
Calling off.
They're in
the second drawer
Nurse,

I swear
I put
them there

Drums stop.

crisp and
white
and

freshly ironed,

folded in
quarters,

just like
Miriam showed,

and smelling
like...
lemons.

She looks down at Pieter lying.

Softly.

This pump
takes
away the pain

does it?

I don't
think
it works
Mr Joubert,

I'll tell
the nurse;

your brow
makes...

creases,

Pause.

And that
tube
feeds you?

You were
better
fat

That's for
sure.

I never
liked your
laugh

Honor
didn't like
your...

tread

your step

in the dark,

your

breath.

I wonder
if you
can hear
me?

I wonder
if you'll
open your
eyes
ever?

I wonder
if you'll

Speak again?

She whispers.

I wonder
if the
journey back
for you

has already

begun?

*Lights change. Drums. BEAUTY looks at the
audience, mischievously, she sets about changing the
scene, pulling the rose bushes about leaving weals in
the earth. With ceremony, she moves the stool.*

Scene 9

Late afternoon, dappled sunshine.

*JENNIFER enters; made-up and coiffeured, elegant in
an African inspired cocktail outfit and large African
jewellery.*

*She is speaking into a mobile phone which is clamped
between her shoulder and ear, and trying to put high
heels on at the same time. She has a dress over one
arm and a tiny bag.*

JENNIFER

It is
a
bad show
a fault

on the line
perhaps
I don't know,

I'll ask Jeffrey
to look at it
tonight
I promise.

Pause.

No change,
they say
he's comfortable
today,
that's something.

No, he can't
eat biscuits

BEAUTY enters briskly, she seems to be en route.

He's not really
drinking
at the moment,

To BEAUTY.

Oh…
dear…

BEAUTY stops.

Into phone.

well, water
of course
but only
a sip

I mean
he's on a
drip!

She throws the dress to BEAUTY.

Into phone.

Prayers?

Pause.

I'm not
sure
Pieter would
want prayers.

I…
I…

I suppose
he would.

I...

Pause.

Goodbye

To BEAUTY.

Now er...

BEAUTY
Beauty

JENNIFER
Oh yes, yes

Tell Jeffrey
the landline
goes straight
onto answer
will you?

That's the
fifth
call on my cell
in half an hour

Of course
it's nice
to know
so many people
care

so many well-wishers

but

it's exhausting
all the same
and...

I can't help
feeling
it's a trifle...

BEAUTY
Spookish?

JENNIFER
Surprised.
Yes,
yes
exactly.

Pause.

BEAUTY
You told Jeffrey
to put
the home phone
straight
to answer
Mrs Joubert

Pause.

JENNIFER
Did I?

BEAUTY
Yes
you worried
that the
phone ringing
all the time
was disturbing
Baas.

You told
Millie you'd
pick up
messages
at night.

JENNIFER
Did I?
Right
Well, I…

I don't remember

She rubs her head.

I don't remember

Pause.

BEAUTY stares at her with naked curiosity – it's almost insolent.

JENNIFER
Sharply.
What are you
looking at?

BEAUTY
… Nothing

Pause.

JENNIFER

You can
have
the dress

I put it
on one side
for Miriam.

It doesn't
suit me now

It will suit
you perfectly.

Pause.

It's linen

Pause.

It's not too
fancy
is it?

A
Sunday dress
I thought

Of course,
I cut off
all the buttons

but
you can sew
can't you?

BEAUTY hands the dress back.

Surprised.

Don't you
want it?

BEAUTY

No, thank you
Mrs Joubert
I don't
want
the dress.

Pause.

JENNIFER

Oh, right.
Right.

Pause.

Are you
going up
to
Mr Joubert?

BEAUTY
Yes.

JENNIFER
Who's sitting
with him?

BEAUTY
The
red-haired
nurse,
with the
big feet.

JENNIFER
Tell her
I'll only be
an hour
or two.

She's got
my
cell phone
number.

BEAUTY
Yes.

JENNIFER
I'm
five minutes
away.

Any change –
she calls me –
those
are her instructions –
tell her

BEAUTY
Right
Pause.

JENNIFER

At least
It's quiet

Pause.

They've gone
the mechanical diggers,
the workmen?

BEAUTY

No

Pause.

JENNIFER

I thought
they had,
I thought
I heard
Millie say
they'd finished
for the day.

BEAUTY

No,
they're still
there.

JENNIFER

Did they
find
anything?

BEAUTY

Yes, yes
they did

Pause.

They did
find something

JENNIFER

Don't tell me
they found
the graves
did they?

Pause.

BEAUTY

They found
a big

grave
yes

a...pit

with many
bodies
in it.

But

they do
not think

these are
the graves
of the
old people.

JENNIFER
What
do you mean?

BEAUTY
It is
not
an ancestral
burial ground
Mrs Joubert.

JENNIFER
No...?

BEAUTY
No...
they
have found
plenty bones

but

in shallow
graves,

not buried
with honour
or respect

some

with their hands
and feet tied

JENNIFER
What?

BEAUTY

Others
with ropes
around their necks

Their heads
In plastic bags

Some
of the bones
are bits

Some are
burnt.

Pause.

JENNIFER

Finding it hard to breathe.
What?

BEAUTY

I said
some
of the bones
are…

JENNIFER

I heard you
I heard you
you…
foolish girl

What
do you think
I'm deaf?

Pause.

JENNIFER is pacing.

How dare you
come in here,
today,
of all days!

How dare you
share
these horrors
in this
abrupt
and…
insolent
way!

Miriam
wouldn't have
done this.

Miriam
would have
spared me.

Where's Miriam?
Where's Miriam?

She is panting.

BEAUTY
Quietly.
Shall I get
Doctor
for you
Mrs Joubert?

JENNIFER
Are
the police
there?

BEAUTY
Yes.

JENNIFER
I saw
the cars

BEAUTY
Also the priests.

JENNIFER
Right.

BEAUTY
They're putting
the bones
in bags,

very careful,
and labelling
them

taking them
back
to the police station.

There are…
forensic people
too

in white coats,
with little brushes
plastic caps,
aprons
and gloves

JENNIFER

Is
everybody watching?

BEAUTY

They've put up
scaffolding
and screens.

JENNIFER

But there's
quite
a little gathering
I bet.

Your friends
and family
must be
delighted.

A
more thrilling
day out
than they'd
bargained for
I'm sure.

I hope
they bought
their primus stoves,

their water's
bubbling
for a brew

Perhaps
Millie
should take out
a tray
of drop scones

I hope
they've got
their
instamatics.

Pause.

BEAUTY
Everybody
is
very quiet
Mrs Joubert

very…
upset.
Pause.

Some people
are angry!

JENNIFER
Angry?

BEAUTY
Yes, angry
Pause.

JENNIFER
Whose are they?
the Bones?

BEAUTY
Do you
want me
to say?

JENNIFER
Yes,
If you know
Yes.

BEAUTY
Jeffrey told us
years ago
this land
used to be
a farm.

JENNIFER
A what?

BEAUTY
An old
farm
Didn't
you know?

JENNIFER

No...
I didn't know
I...

I
didn't
know

BEAUTY

That p'raps
out on the edge
of the farm
there was
a bad place

an out-house
an old cattle stall

quite big.

Police
brought our people
here,
from the police station
many years ago
to question them
where their
screams
could not
be heard

to torture them
to kill them

Sometimes
they
burnt the flesh
then
buried the bones

in a pit behind
where the soil
was soft
and didn't
take much digging

Away from
prying eyes.

Pause, JENNIFER is pacing.

JENNIFER
Jeffrey told you this?

BEAUTY
Jeffrey
is
very old.

JENNIFER
Jeffrey
knew
of this?

BEAUTY
Yes,
Jeffrey knew
and the old folk too.

Pause.

JENNIFER puts her hands over her head, she sinks to the ground.

BEAUTY watches.

JENNIFER
Such a…
long time.

Such a
very long
time.

Pause.

JENNIFER is still.

Then, quite suddenly, she stands, dusts herself down. From her little bag she takes out a compact, she fixes her hair.

BEAUTY watches.

From off stage, there is a sudden commotion, doors opening, raised voices, shouting.

Softly.

Go and see
what that
commotion
is about

will you
Beauty?

BEAUTY leaves. JENNIFER stands, completely still.

Pause.

BEAUTY rushes back in.

BEAUTY

Come quick

It's Mr Joubert.

He's
stopped
breathing.

Drums. BEAUTY changes the scene, pulling the bags she recreates the bed.

Scene 10

Lights change, shadows, coming to dusk. Drumming stops.

Outside, but close by, a massing crowd, occasionally singing, spontaneous prayer.

JENNIFER sits by Pieter's bed, her shoulders slumped, her hands clasped in her lap. She strains forward, looking intently at Pieter. She is breathing heavily.

BEAUTY enters.

BEAUTY

Softly.

Mrs Joubert

JENNIFER

Yes.

BEAUTY

Millie
sent me
to say

Miss Dottie
rang
for the fifth time
today.

She said
if she
couldn't
speak to
you
on the
telephone

she planned
to come
in person.

JENNIFER
Distressed.
No, no.
I won't see
anyone.

You hear

talk
to
anyone

I have
to be
alone.

BEAUTY
Millie
told her
the Baas
was still
holding on –

just,

but

worse

that you
thanked
everyone
for their
good wishes,

but…

Pause.

JENNIFER
Yes…?

Pause.

BEAUTY
I forget
The rest.

JENNIFER laughs, softly.

JENNIFER
And outside?

BEAUTY
Outside?

JENNIFER
Yes

BEAUTY
The crowd
is
getting
bigger.
Pause.

JENNIFER
Stands…snapping.
Tell Jeffrey
to call
the police.

BEAUTY
But…

JENNIFER
Now,
do you
hear me?

BEAUTY
I…

JENNIFER
I don't
want
excuses,

it's
outrageous;

my husband,
my…
darling husband
of forty-two years

is dying,

tonight
perhaps
I'm kindly
told.

Doesn't
he deserve

some peace
and quiet?

BEAUTY
Mrs Joubert.

JENNIFER
They're
on my
property –

virtually,

almost
in my
garden –

anyway,

making
a nuisance
of themselves –

certainly.

I'm told
they're at
the front gate
now.

Cars
can hardly
get in
or out

I'm under
siege.

It's upsetting,
deeply upsetting –

I find their
presence…
threatening.

Call the police.

BEAUTY
But,
Mrs Joubert
the police
are here…

JENNIFER
Here?

BEAUTY

Yes
10
or 20
of them
at least

They have
built platforms
to view
the bones
in the pit.

They have
set up
floodlights

and one or two
take pictures
now with
flash cameras
at dusk.

JENNIFER

Why?

BEAUTY

Because
it is
a
'crime scene'.

JENNIFER

What?

BEAUTY

So you see

if you
wish to
speak to
the police

all you have
to do
is to go
downstairs
through the kitchen
onto
the patio
and step into
your garden.

Pause.

JENNIFER

Starts to cry.

I'm frightened.

What
if they
decide
to climb
the fence?

BEAUTY

They'd be
electrocuted.

JENNIFER

Dig
under the
palisade?

BEAUTY

The same.

JENNIFER

You say
there's
ten or twenty
police

but

they're
outnumbered.

There are
hundreds
out there
I am told,

maybe
thousands:

they could
charge
the gate
and
kill us
every one.

It's happened
before
I'm sure
I know.

Pause.

BEAUTY
The crowd
sing
that's all

sway
and moan
perhaps.

Sometimes
they pray

An old man
an oupa

is carried
on his
grandson's back;

and as
each
bag of bones
comes up

he sighs;
so does
his neighbour,
and the next.

Sighs,
passed

are good
for easing
troubled
souls

JENNIFER
You speak
to
the dead

you said.

BEAUTY
The spirits
yes…

JENNIFER
Well…
tell the spirits
to send

the crowd
away.

BEAUTY
I'm sorry

JENNIFER
Make
them go,

the old grandpa
the women
in
their best
frocks
the men
in hats
the children

make them go.

Pause.

I'll pay you
I'll pay you
very well

Four thousand rand

A tinkling sound.

Pause.

BEAUTY
Eight thousand rand

A louder tinkling.

Pause.

It is
a
big crowd,

JENNIFER
Eight thousand rand?

BEAUTY
What
if the spirits
want
the crowd
to stay?

JENNIFER
Don't you know

if
that's the case?

BEAUTY

Of course not.
How would
I know that?

I haven't
spoken to them
yet.

Pause.

I will charge
Four thousand rand
down payment

which is
reasonable
indeed

for troubled
souls

who are
more difficult
to reach,
like these,

and who
don't like
to speak.

Another four thousand
if I get
the crowd
to go

What do you say?

JENNIFER

Anything.

BEAUTY

And no
cheques
please.

JENNIFER

There's cash
in the drawer
there,
I don't know
how much.

BEAUTY

I trust you
Mrs Joubert

The crowd gets louder.

JENNIFER

Agonised.

Quick, please
you have
to help
me,
do you
hear?
They can't
be
out
there
when
my poor husband
dies.

You have
to make
them go

The crowd gets louder, closer.

BEAUTY

I don't know
Mrs Joubert
it will take
powerful magic

against
so many
living souls

made strong
by
one another

JENNIFER

Please

BEAUTY

I'll need
your help
to reach
the spirits

JENNIFER
Anything
Anything

BEAUTY
Hold
my hand

JENNIFER
Your hand?

BEAUTY
Yes,
both my hands.

The crowd gets louder.

JENNIFER holds BEAUTY's hands.

We have
to close
our eyes

and breathe
as one

feel
the rhythm
of our breath
through fingers

In –

and

out

like this.

They breathe together.

*BEAUTY jerks back her head, the drums accompany,
JENNIFER opens her eyes and watches. BEAUTY
stiffens, her eyes roll in her head. She starts to speak
'in tongues'. It is a version of Xhosa. It is exotic,
impressive and a bit scary. She appears to be asking
questions in one voice, answering in another.*

*She speaks, louder and faster and more ferocious.
She drops hands with JENNIFER, her whole body
is shaking, the movements, seemingly involuntary,
become a kind of dance.*

Light change – darker as the sun goes down.

*Outside the crowds are starting to sound softer, and
far away.*

The crowds are dispersing.

BEAUTY's 'dance' starts to wind down, softer and softer, she is drenched in sweat, exhausted, almost falling over.

Drumming stops.

JENNIFER
Are they leaving?

Pause.

Incredulous.

They're leaving!

I think
they're
leaving.

JENNIFER is sick with relief, trembling, ecstatic.

You did it

You made
them go.

BEAUTY
Hoarse.
The spirits
said
the eyes
had seen
enough.

JENNIFER
So
you have
power?

BEAUTY
Yes

JENNIFER
Truly.

BEAUTY
Truly

JENNIFER
Heal my husband.

I will
pay you
anything
you ask

BEAUTY
Anything?

Pause.

JENNIFER
You like
this house
don't you,
Beauty?

BEAUTY
Yes, I
like this
house
very much

JENNIFER
I
will give
you
this house

if you can heal
my husband.

Drumming.

Scene 11

JENNIFER is by Pieter's bedside. She paces. Absolute silence.

JENNIFER
They're gone
darling,

The wailing
crowds

Silently

and

orderly.

It's...
miraculous.

Pause.

This

girl

is

miraculous.

Pause.

She paces.

Remember
that
Christmas

We'd been
married
just
five years,

and trying
for a
baby

all that
time,

I was so
sad

So
you sent
everyone
away –

everyone.

You cooked
Christmas dinner,
turkey
and all
the trimmings

You
rubbed
salt
and cider
into the
turkey
skin

to make
it specially
brown
and crispy…

specially juicy,

I laughed
at you,
remember,

Piet?

in your
funny
chef's hat
and
frilly apron –

for
the first time
in months
I laughed

We
picnicked

in the garden
by the pool
under a
jacaranda
tree.

You laid
a cloth

on the
hot
grass,

I started
to freckle
in the
sun

you draped
your towel
over my
shoulders,

we drank
ice cold
champagne

and
afterwards

well
you remember
what happened
afterwards

Remember
Piet?

We'd

been married
five years.

Pause.

She paces.

I was
always

too…

curious

wasn't I?

with
my
fairy questions

I couldn't
wait
at home

like all
the other

fairy wives

wait

safe inside…

BEAUTY bustles in, without ceremony; she has a shopping bag.

BEAUTY
Excuse me
Mrs Joubert.

JENNIFER
You
startled
me!

BEAUTY
We have
to rush,

a cloud
has just
passed
by the
bright
full moon

leaving
a trail

of two
goat's horns

JENNIFER
Is that good?

BEAUTY
Don't ask me
I can't
read clouds.

They are
a
big mystery.

Children
read clouds best,

girl children
under three
are
world experts
I believe…

Now –

She takes out a small wooden pot from her bag.

JENNIFER
What's that?

BEAUTY
You mustn't
ask
so many
questions
Mrs Joubert.

It stops
the magic.

BEAUTY removes the lid and takes a pinch of white powder.

Drumming.

She starts to hum, and then to intone a note. She sprinkles the white powder at arms' length, all over Pieter in the bed, from head to toe.

BEAUTY speaks/incants 'in tongues'; it is Xhosa-sounding but different, she is very focused.

Drumming stops.

There

She is sweating.

Where
does the
good doctor
think
his
sickness…
stems?

JENNIFER
The brain,
he has
a
tumour
in his
brain

they tried
to
cut it out
and he
went blind.

The oxygen
is keeping
him alive

He hardly
moves,
but he
can hear

we think.

BEAUTY
And speak?

JENNIFER
He hasn't
spoken now
for several
weeks

BEAUTY
He seems
to sleep
deep
and
dreamless.

JENNIFER
That's
the drugs.

BEAUTY
Mrs Joubert
I have
to hold
Mr Joubert's
head.

Do
you mind?

JENNIFER
Anything.

BEAUTY holds his head.

Pieter's eyes open suddenly.

Drum rattle.

They jump.

Darling…
Darling…!

We're here
You're safe.

BEAUTY
His breath
is short
and fast.

JENNIFER
I'm here.

BEAUTY
His spirit
calls you.

BEAUTY connects with his open eyes. Drumming. She speaks soft and low 'in tongues'. Finally she stops.

Drumming stops.

JENNIFER
You've brought
colour
to his cheeks

Who'd
have thought
it?

To his
soft
lips.

BEAUTY
And look –
his
blind eyes
hold
memory.

JENNIFER
Yes.

BEAUTY
Softly.
His
grey
glass eyes.

BEAUTY is still holding his head. She starts to move his head in her hands as if involuntarily, like a water dowser.

Drumming

She stops, let the head go.

She slumps, as if exhausted.

Then, her head bowed, she starts to incant intensely. Her hands trace all of Pieter's body, in the air, and sometimes the hands seem to meet resistance, forcing them up, and BEAUTY has to aggressively press down. This happens especially over the head, they eyes and the mouth.

Drumming stops.

Silence and stillness.

BEAUTY stars intently into Pieter's eyes.

She puts one hand to his right ear and from it pulls out a long rat's tail.

Triumphant, exhausted.

Got it!
See!
I got it!

JENNIFER
Aghast.
Oh

my God
what
is it?

BEAUTY
The tail
of
a rat!

The Baas's
pain
is because
he has a
rat
gnawing
at his brain.

See,
here's the
tail.

One dark
night

rats
copulated
and the rat egg
rolled into his
ear.

The
infant rat
is still
in there

it gnaws
his skull

nibbles
his brain

into
a
bloody
ragged
mess.

JENNIFER
Rising hysteria.
No, no
this is

...

nonsense.

No.

I...

Go away

No!

BEAUTY
Quick

we have
to move
him
to the
pit!

JENNIFER
The pit?

BEAUTY
Where
the bones
are buried.

JENNIFER
The bones?

BEAUTY
Yes.

JENNIFER
Why?

BEAUTY
I don't
know why.

Except his
tormented
spirit
tells me to
take
his body
there.

JENNIFER
No...
it isn't
possible,

anyway
the shame.

I'd rather
let him
die
here in bed

I'd rather…

BEAUTY
There is
another way

JENNIFER
Well…?

BEAUTY
Take a
clipping
of his hair
nail
and
a scrape
of spit

down
to the pit

and exorcise
the evil things
he did
in life.

JENNIFER
Soft, trembling.
Evil?

BEAUTY
Firmly.
Yes.
Evil.

JENNIFER
I…
I don't
know
what
you mean

BEAUTY
Don't you?

JENNIFER
No
you talk
…
nonsense
…
mischief

And it's
impertinent

It…
frightens
me

BEAUTY
His spirit
Speaks,
his
troubled
spirit

JENNIFER
Will this
make
my husband well?

BEAUTY
Well?

JENNIFER
Will
he live?

BEAUTY
I'm sorry
Mrs Joubert

You don't
understand.

Keeping him
alive

is not
the
job now.

JENNIFER
No?

BEAUTY

We battle
for
his soul

JENNIFER

His soul?

BEAUTY

And
one thing's
sure,

if we
don't
obey
his spirit

his
tormented
soul
will be
gnawed
by the
Devil-rats
into an
agonised eternity!

JENNIFER

Pacing.
A lock
of hair?

BEAUTY

A nail
and

spit!

*Breath – tinkling sounds. Singing – the Isinyanya
come closer.*

Scene 12

The pit, a broad beam of a floodlight.
*BEAUTY and JENNIFER arrive via the viewing
platform.*
They whisper.

JENNIFER
My poor

rose garden…

BEAUTY
It's smaller
than
I thought…

JENNIFER
How deep
is it?

BEAUTY
and shallower

JENNIFER
I can't
see
properly
in the
dark…

BEAUTY
Not
deep
at all

It's as if
they tossed
the bodies
in

like trash

JENNIFER whimpers.

To cast
my spell

You must
climb down
to the
bottom
of the
pit,

and mix
with
the soil

the Baas's
hair, nail
and spit.

JENNIFER
I can't,
I'm afraid,

I can't
climb down

it's
preposterous
at my age,

I'm scared
They've left…

things
down there.

BEAUTY
Things?

JENNIFER
More…

BEAUTY
Horrors.

JENNIFER
Yes.

BEAUTY
The small
bone
of a finger
p'raps,

JENNIFER
Don't, please.

BEAUTY
A toe,

A tooth!
Pause.

JENNIFER
You'll have
to do
it.

BEAUTY
What?

JENNIFER
I'm paying

you
aren't I?
I
order you.

BEAUTY
It
won't work
through me

Mrs Joubert.

To exorcise
the evil
Mr Joubert
did in life

it has
to be
his wife.

JENNIFER
Evil again!

BEAUTY
You must
seek
forgiveness
for him

in the pit.

That's what
his
sleeping spirit
says

JENNIFER
Forgiveness,
from whom?

BEAUTY
Don't you
know?

Pause. JENNIFER stares at BEAUTY.

JENNIFER
Stifled, desperate.
All right,
I'll do it
All right.

*Gingerly, and very slowly, JENNIFER starts to shin
down into the pit. A tinkling sound.*

*She is panting, whimpering, shaking; BEAUTY
watches.*

BEAUTY
Best not
disturb
the soil
too much.

JENNIFER
I'm
trying
not to

but,

it's as
dry
as dust.

BEAUTY
Surprised.
And smells
of rain.

JENNIFER
Looking up.
Look!

A drum rattle.

BEAUTY
Looking in the same direction.
What?

JENNIFER
In the
far distance,
on the hill
two figures
the warriors
from my dream.

Can
you see
them?

BEAUTY looks.

The man,
and the
fierce
robed woman
with a spear.

BEAUTY
Humouring her.
Oh yes.

JENNIFER
Who
are they?

BEAUTY
Don't you
know?

JENNIFER shakes her head.

They are
our
ancestors

come

to protect
the bones
of the
Isinyanya
in the pit,

from

scavengers.

JENNIFER
Whispers.
Do they
think
I'm a
scavenger?

BEAUTY
Yes!

JENNIFER shakes.

We must
be quick.

Take the
hair first

In your palms.

JENNIFER

Like this?

BEAUTY

Just
like that,

exactly
like
that.

*BEAUTY stiffens, her eyes glaze, she starts to sway,
and wails as if in pain, this then turns into a
terrifying song. Then:*

Bury
his hair
in the
earth.

JENNIFER does so. A tinkling sound.

Do
you feel
the
sudden
heat?

JENNIFER

Yes
Yes.
Don't let me
be
burnt alive!

BEAUTY

Quick,
take the nail
now,
and
plant it
like a seed.

JENNIFER does so. A tinkling.

Place
the scrape
of spit

next to
your

heart.

BEAUTY starts to hum, she seems to 'grow'
– possessed by the spirits.

Drumming.

JENNIFER watches terrified.

In gruff, spirit voice.
You're back.

In her own voice.
He thinks
you've
been here
before.

JENNIFER
Who
is
he?

BEAUTY
I'm
not sure,
some ancestor
or other,

a big
knob

on
the other
side.

JENNIFER says nothing.

In gruff spirit voice.
Answer
me!

JENNIFER
Softly.
Yes…
yes…
I'm back.

BEAUTY
In gruff ancestor's voice.
You mean
back
in your
rose garden?

JENNIFER

I think
p'raps
I was
here before

long
long
ago

though
I'm not
sure.

Here,
or
hereabouts

one

dreadful

night.

BEAUTY

Curious, her own voice.
You have
to tell
the spirit.

JENNIFER

Gently, weakly.
Do I?

BEAUTY

Curiously.
Yes.

JENNIFER

Weak, strange.
Yes,
I have to
after all
these years,

I have to,
I have to,

finally –

to save
my husband's

soul.

BEAUTY

Softly.
And
perhaps
your soul
Mrs Joubert.

JENNIFER

Pieter and I
had been
married

5 years,
5 happy years,

we'd been
trying
for
a baby
without luck,

but then

I conceived
one Christmas
and
we were
so happy
both
of us

looking forward
to being
a
real family
at last.

Pause.

Pieter worked
long hours

at the
police station,

always
had done,

his work
often
seemed to
go on
long

into the
evening,

through
the night
sometimes

he'd come
back
in the
early hours,
I'd wake
to
the patter
of the
downstairs
shower

He'd fall
into bed
smelling
of soap
and…
eucalyptus

BEAUTY
What
of his
clothes?

JENNIFER
He'd put
them out
for
the girl
to wash

Pause.

He had
a couple
of
special friends.

I didn't
like
these men.

Every evening
after a few
beers,

they'd

head off
together
to some
place
or other –

following
tip-offs,
Piet said,
pursuing
leads,

standard
police cop
stuff.

'No need
to bother
your
pretty head

Jenny Wren.'

I was 23
and
pregnant.

I wanted
my husband
home
at night.

I worried.

Perhaps,

they were
going
to bars

BEAUTY
Picking up
women.

JENNIFER
Yes.

Pause.

Of course

Yes.

One night
I borrowed
a friend's

old car.

A car
I knew
Pieter
wouldn't
recognise.

I waited
in the
car park

of the

Sports Bar
on Bonsile
Street.

When they
came out,
the three
of them,

all merry –

I followed
keeping
a safe distance,

careful,
sly even,
in disguise
hat, glasses,
coat.

I smiled
at
the funny
stranger
in the
car mirror.

They went
back to the
police station

and after
15 minutes
came out
through
a back door

dragging –
kicking
and screaming

a young
black boy –

stuffed him
into
the car boot

and then
drove off
into the night.

I should
have gone
back home,

he wasn't
seeing
women
after all,

but

I was curious
about my
husband's
work,

about
his secret
life.

I wanted
to see

what kept
him
from me

night
after
night,
after night

and so
I
followed.

Pause.

They drove
to an
old farm,

Not too
far
from home

about 20 miles
that's all

but

it was
dark

and the
road
twisted

And quickly
I was
lost

I turned
off
a side road

more
of a
dirt track

and waited
where
I could
look out

waited
for them
to come
back.

I waited
hours.

I don't know
why.

Anyway,
I fell asleep

and when
I woke
It was late –

3 a m

I was
sure
Pieter
was still
there.

I thought
I must

go home now.

I'll stop
Someone,
someone
respectable

Ask
where
I am

If I leave
straight away
I'll be back
before him,
get into bed,

ruffle my hair,
pretend
I'd been there
all night.

But instead
I got out
of the car,
and walked
silently
trying not to
snap twigs
underfoot

up the track,
past the deserted
farmhouse

to where
his car
was parked.

Pause.

I could
hear my
heart
thump.

A dim
green light
came
from what
looked like

an old
cattle stall.

For some reason,
I don't know
why,
I don't know
why
to this day,

I stepped
inside.

It was big
and bare,
smelling of
straw.

There was
no one
there,

that's what
I thought
at first.

Then
I heard
a drip drip
sound,

steady
and rhythmic.

I looked up.

Suspended
from
the ceiling

tied with rope

was the
young
black boy,

his belly
exposed,

whipped
into
a piece
of
raw meat

and

the dripping
was

his blood,

which

made a

sickly pool

on

the

straw floor.

I couldn't

scream.

His eyes

looked at

me.

He spoke –

I think

he spoke –

I think

I…

can't remember

if he spoke.

Did we

speak?

I heard

footsteps,

voices…

Pieter's voice.

I slipped

into

the shadows,

squatted

on my

haunches

in a

cattle stall.

The black

boy's

eyes

must have

followed

me,

I think

but they

didn't
see
me

as they
cut
him down

groaning

and dragged
him out
into
the dark

still
I didn't
move.

I heard
fire crackling,

and saw

flame
dancing
shadows.

There was
one
last bout
of
terrible screams

and then

silence.

Pause.

After a while
they
came back

in

and
sat down
on
hay bales

I heard
them…

Pause.

This
I have

tried hard
to forget

this
I can
hardly
say

I heard them

open beers

I swear

laughing,

joking…

joking…

and it…
went on

for what
seemed
to me,
to be
eternity.

Pause.

What's that
terrible
smell?

BEAUTY
Burning flesh
is it?

JENNIFER
I was
calm
at first

quite calm,

trying not
to breathe.

I thought
they'll be
gone soon

off in
the
car.

Pieter will
be worried

when he
finds I'm
not at
home.

I'll get
Janey
to ring

say

I felt
a bit
unwell
that day,

decided

to stay
the night.

They won't
find
the car
parked
in the
lane.

All
I had
to do

was wait,

stay still
and quiet

and everything
could have
gone on

perfect
as before,

but

the air
was dry
with dust
from the

straw,

and I
sneezed.

Pause.

BEAUTY

Go on
Mrs Joubert.

Finish your
story
please.

JENNIFER

Pieter sent
the men
away.

He asked
me
what I'd
seen.

I told
him.

We walked
together
to his
car.

He said
he'd send
a rookie
to pick up
Pat's car
In the lane
tomorrow.

He didn't
hold
my hand.

His face
was
very pale

like wax,

covered in
beads of
sweat

bubbles

of

sweat.

I realised
I had

seen
this man's
wax face

before

but not
the dead
glass eyes.

He didn't
shower

He didn't
change
his clothes

He slept
downstairs
on the
big settee.

I begged
him
to come
to bed.

He cursed,
then cried,

told me
the black boy

was bad
all through,

a bad
lot,

that
he'd tried to
inform

against
some good
cops;

that he
was withholding

valuable
information,

he knew
names,

top names

of rebel

parties

responsible
for

serious insurrection
in
the townships.

He
became

very angry
with
the bad
black boy.

Pause.

All the time
pouring
whisky

from a
crystal
decanter

into an
English
teacup,

drinking
cup
after
cup.

He told
me
in a
strange
voice

a voice
I hadn't
heard
before

I swear

he told
me
and I've
tried
so hard

to
forget this

so hard

for so
long

but
I couldn't…
I can't
forget this

he
told me
a body
took about
7 hours
to burn,

he'd often
gone back
he said

and found

the buttocks

still roasting.

'Imagine that'

he said

and laughed.

He laughed.

Pause.

I miscarried
that night,

nothing
dramatic
you understand,

cramps
blood and
a blob
of jelly

in the
upstairs
toilet.

Pause.

Next morning
he went back,

I know
because
he told me.

He went
back
to bury
the
black boy's
bones
with other bones
and
bodies
in the pit

from
other nights.

Of course
I must
never speak
of what
I saw
he said,
as if I would

Pause.

Pieter never
slept
with me
again.

To my
shame
that was
his choice
not mine.

BEAUTY looks astonished.

That
surprises
you?

BEAUTY
No, Mrs Joubert,
horrifies me.

JENNIFER
He was
my husband

and I
loved him

Pause.

BEAUTY
Then
your husband
was a
devil

JENNIFER
I loved him
so much

BEAUTY
Then,
you loved
the Devil.

Pause.

JENNIFER
Will he
be
forgiven?

BEAUTY
Sorry?

JENNIFER
The spell.
I'm paying
you
to cast
a spell
to save
his soul
from hell

remember?

BEAUTY
Softly.
Oh yes
I remember now,
Eternal and Agonising
Hell.

JENNIFER
Well… ?

Long pause.

BEAUTY
There
is no
spell

Mrs Joubert.

Pause.

JENNIFER
What?

BEAUTY
Oh,
it's quite
true

I was
born
at the
very hour

my
grandfather
died.

It's true
my Xhosa
name
means
forefather's
voice

but sadly

I am
a
disappointment
to
my mother

I
was not
born
with the
caul.

I have
never
been
in touch

with ancestors,

spirits,
ghosts or

spookies

of

any

description.

I

cannot

cast

spells.

I

do not

believe

in magic.

I have

no

supernatural

powers

In fact

as

human beings

go

I

might appear

to be

pretty

powerless

Mrs Joubert.

JENNIFER

No
No!

BEAUTY

But

it seems
to me
if ever

there was
a
dying soul
condemned
to
eternal

hell
and suffering
it is
that
wretched man

your husband.

JENNIFER
You have
power.

BEAUTY
No.
I am
a
fraud.

JENNIFER
I saw
you
send
the crowd
away.

BEAUTY
A
trickster.

JENNIFER
Five hundred
strong,
they left
at your
command.

BEAUTY
Laughing.
It was dusk.

I know
the ways
of
our people.

At
the very
moment

when
the sun

sets
they leave
a burial site.

To stay
is
disrespectful,

to stay
means
mischief.

Pause.

JENNIFER
The tail –
the rat's
tail!

BEAUTY
What
about it?

JENNIFER
I saw
you
draw it
from
my husband's
ear.

BEAUTY
You are
a
foolish
woman.

If

you really
believe
a rat
nibbles
your husband's
brain?

JENNIFER
I thought
It was
magic…
I thought

it was…

a metaphor…

BEAUTY laughs.

a…

psychic
manifestation…

BEAUTY laughs louder.

I thought
it was
black magic.

BEAUTY
Laughing.
A simple
conjuring
trick.

JENNIFER
Why?

BEAUTY
To make
money
Mrs Joubert.

I have
established
a
successful
little
healing practice

The men
of course
don't like
a girl
Isangomo

In fact
they
hate it

And would
have me
destroyed

But
my successes
spread

by word
of mouth

satisfied
customers
tell their
sick
and troubled
friends

who beg
me
to make
all well.

Today
was a
particularly
successful
day

I earned

Eight thousand rand.

That is
three months
maid's salary.

Pause.

I have
no intention
of spending
my life
in a
township
shack,

dusting

a silly

white woman's
expensive knickknacks.

Pause.

JENNIFER
Why bring
me here?

BEAUTY
To the
pit?

JENNIFER
Yes.

BEAUTY
At
the dead
of night?

JENNIFER
Yes!

BEAUTY
I think
you
deserved it!

Pause.

JENNIFER
You
must give
me
the money
back

d'you hear?

I am
not
a rich woman
anymore.

BEAUTY
No
Mrs Joubert

Indeed
I think
you should
pay double
for my time

another
eight thousand rand
if you
please.

Pause.

JENNIFER paces.

JENNIFER
Or
you'll tell

people
I suppose.

BEAUTY

Astonished.
Tell
people?

Everyone
already
knows!

JENNIFER

Knows?
Knows what?

BEAUTY

That
the Baas
used to
beat our
brothers
and our sons,
torture
them

to death;

sometimes
in
police stations

sometimes
at night

in

evil places;

that when
the commission
people

tried
to call him
to account

he fled,

you fled
together
for a while.

JENNIFER

How dare
they
inflict
their
rough justice
on us!

Try to
humiliate
and
shame us.

Don't they
know

how we

suffered!

all these
years.

How I
suffered

Truly!

Long pause.

BEAUTY looks incredulous. She laughs.

BEAUTY

How
did you
suffer?

JENNIFER

For the last
thirty-seven years
my life
has been
a hateful sham

Pause.

Can you
imagine,

sitting opposite
each other
at the breakfast
table,

letting

the wireless

fill
the silence

opening
mail

discussing
share prices

Dottie's
Tummy tuck

Steve's
Drink problem.

Living together
like
polite shadows

our
lost love a
ghost
between us.

One time
his hand
brushed mine
accidentally
underneath
the table,

he snatched
it away
as if scalded.

BEAUTY
Why
didn't you
leave him?

JENNIFER
I couldn't
I felt…

sorry…
for him.

BEAUTY
Sorry?

JENNIFER
He
was so
ashamed

BEAUTY

Ashamed
of what
he'd done?

Pause.

JENNIFER

Ashamed
of what
I'd seen

BEAUTY

After that
night,
did the
killing and torture
continue?

Pause, JENNIFER paces.

JENNIFER

Yes.

I had
years
waiting
for him
to come
home

with

blood
on
his shoes,

I suppose

smelling
of
burnt black
flesh

and
death

I imagine

always
making for

the
cut glass decanter,

swigging

whisky

from an

English teacup.

BEAUTY
Most people
think
your husband
enjoyed
hurting
our people.
Pause.

JENNIFER
Softly.
Maybe

BEAUTY
My God!

JENNIFER
I don't know

BEAUTY
You never
asked him
Pause.

JENNIFER
No.
I never
asked
Pause.

BEAUTY
But you
stayed
married
to this
man.

JENNIFER
I told
you
I had
no choice

BEAUTY

Very angry.

No
Mrs Joubert
you had
a choice.

You had
a
choice!

You had
a
choice!

JENNIFER

I paid
the price
didn't I?
I paid
with thirty-seven
precious
years of
life.

I paid
with
my life

Listening
every night
in
my dreams
to that
poor boy's
screams
of agony

Listening
to him
plead

plead
with me

to save
his
life.

Pause.

Something is happening to BEAUTY, her body is in
the throes of a strange force. Contractions rack her
body, wave after wave. She is screaming, but silently.

What is it?

What's happening?

What's happening
to you?

BEAUTY's body twists and contorts, as if in agony.

A sudden anguished silence, stillness.

Then.

A drip, drip sound, from the drum.

BEAUTY *AS BOY*
Help me.
Help me

please

Help me

JENNIFER
I...
I don't
know
how

BEAUTY *AS BOY*
Cut me down

Cut me down

JENNIFER
I
cut you
down

BEAUTY *AS BOY*
Untie me
Untie my
hands

JENNIFER
Yes
Yes
untie your
hands

BEAUTY *AS BOY*
My feet,
untie me

JENNIFER

Yes,
yes.
Your feet
yes

Drumming. BEAUTY as the BOY starts to untwist. It is strange, like a dance.

Finally he stands tall. JENNIFER and the BOY stare at each other.

Drumming stops.

Pause.

BEAUTY *AS BOY*

You've changed

JENNIFER

Yes
I have
changed

BEAUTY *AS BOY*

Where
is the
wide-eyed
fair-haired
girl
in sandals?

JENNIFER

Gone

BEAUTY *AS BOY*

It's strange
to have
flesh
on my bones.

Pause.

JENNIFER

Can you
forgive me?

Pause.

BEAUTY *AS BOY*

Yes

JENNIFER

She is crying.

How?

When I
can't
forgive
myself.

Pause.

Can you
forgive
him?

BEAUTY *AS BOY*

I met
under the soil

brothers:

one died
with
'Nimi'
on his
blue lips

this was

his
sweetheart's

name.

One
felt his
sister's
sweet breath
on his neck
whispering
girls' secrets;

another,
in the silence
between
the crack
of the
horse whip

heard his
mother call

and
another
and

another
and
all
the others

But

the last
thing
we all saw

before

the end
through
black blood
was
your husband's

grey glass
eyes.

Pause.

JENNIFER
Can you
forgive
him?

Blackout.

Drumming, singing. The bones speak.

Scene 13

BEAUTY and JENNIFER. They sit together in the audience, between them the musician, who drums softly through the scene. They look at the empty stage.

JENNIFER
He's dead.

BEAUTY
Who?

JENNIFER
My
husband.

BEAUTY
Is he?

JENNIFER nods.

How
do you
know?

JENNIFER
I
feel it

BEAUTY
Yes
I feel
it too!

At last.
We have
all waited
a long time
for that
man
to die.

Pause.

And the
boy
lives
it seems
through
me

She laughs.

It would
appear

I have
the caul
after all.

Pause.

JENNIFER
I knew
you were
powerful

Pause.

BEAUTY
What
will you
do?

JENNIFER
Do?

BEAUTY
Yes
do now
with your
life?
Now
you are
free

JENNIFER
I don't
know
I like
to collect
things

BEAUTY
They
collect
dust

JENNIFER
I like
to grow
things

They both look at the land.

BEAUTY
I don't
want
the roses
back

JENNIFER
No

BEAUTY
They're
greedy
for
water

JENNIFER
What kind
of garden

would you
like?

BEAUTY
I would
like big
pink flowers

JENNIFER
Bougainvillea?

BEAUTY
I don't
know
their name

JENNIFER
They're greedy
for water
too

BEAUTY
And the
creeping
purple ones

JENNIFER
Bolusanthus?

BEAUTY
Yes
I will have
a lot
of
Bolusanthus

JENNIFER
You'll need
some ground
cover

BEAUTY
Will I?

JENNIFER
Hypoxis?

BEAUTY
What
for shade?

JENNIFER

A Cestus
Africana

BEAUTY

And I
will
plant a stone
for every
lost
and tortured
soul

JENNIFER

Or Lithops
which are
living stones
flowers spring
from
cracks

*Long, long pause. The drumming louder and more
vibrant, then suddenly stops.*

What
are your
plans

for

the

house?

Blackout.

*Drumming and singing. The Isinyanya and the bones
rejoice.*